Elegant Porcelain & Glass Painting Projects

BY CARIN HEIDEN ATKINS

NORTH LIGHT BOOKS
CINCINNATI, OHIO
www.northlight.com

About the *Author*

A passion for living and living well dictates the work of Carin Heiden Atkins. A self-taught artist, Carin has had work featured on several television programs, such as *Leeza* (NBC), *Home and Family* (The Family Channel) and *Home Green Home* (PBS). Her work has also appeared in many magazines, including *Handcraft Illustrated*, *Arts & Crafts*, *Painting*, *Craftworks*, *Paintworks*, and *Decorating Digest*. When she is not painting on glass and porcelain, Carin enjoys interior design, gardening, traveling, silk painting, calligraphy, floral design and spending time with her family.

04 03 02 01 00 5 4 3 2 1

Library of Congress Cataloging-in-Publication Data

Atkins, Carin Heiden
    Elegant glass and porcelain painting projects / by Carin Heiden Atkins
       p. cm.
    ISBN 1-58180-079-7 (alk.paper)
    1. Glass painting and staining. 2. China painting. I. Title

 TT298 .A88 2000
 748.5'028'2–dc21

                                                 00-040099

Editors: Nicole Klungle and Tricia Waddell
Designer: Amy D. Hawk
Cover designer: Karla Stover
Production coordinator: Sara Dumford
Photographers: Christine Polomsky and Al Parrish

Acknowledgments

Many, Many, Many Thanks!

This book would not have been possible without the tremendous talent and great support of many people. To my wonderful husband David, thanks for your love, support, great cheerleading ability and for coping with the charms of being married to an artist. To my parents and sister, Bill, Drinda and Erica, somehow thank you will never be enough. Thank you for instilling in me the confidence and strength of character I needed to accomplish my dreams. To my wonderful grandparents, Glen and Sylvia, your enthusiastic support of my efforts has kept me striving forward. I am truly grateful to have you both in my life. Thank you to Steve Atkins for his advice and assistance. A great big thank-you also to Bob and Marcia Harris for being so incredibly supportive of my work and creativity.

To my North Light Books family, thank you for believing in me from the very beginning! My superb and wonderful editor Nicole Klungle sought me out, and I am grateful for her fortitude in guiding this project. Nicole has become a true friend indeed, and my most humble thanks will never be enough. Jane Friedman, thank you for all of your behind-the-scenes work. Christine Polomsky, thank you for your photography. And last but certainly not least, Greg Albert, thank you for allowing me to accomplish my dreams by writing this book and for assembling a wonderfully talented and delightful group of people to work with. This whole experience has been wonderful.

To all of the wonderful manufacturers who supported my efforts in this book, I offer my most grateful thank-you! Thank you to the paint companies including Pébéo of America (Angela and Yves), Delta Technical Coatings (Shea, Debbie and Barbie), Liquitex–Binney & Smith (Heidi), Duncan (Lynn and Lee), DecoArt (Pam, Etta and Doxie), EK Success (Dale) and Plaid (Jean, Lauren and Debra). Brushes and painting accessories were graciously given by Loew-Cornell (Shirley), and colour shapers by Forsline and Starr (Rachel and Ladd). Some surfaces were provided by Industrial Can Company (Jan).

22

92

96

Table of Contents

Projects

54

44

Introduction

If you ask me, glass and porcelain painting is one of the easiest crafts to become involved in and addicted to. When I started painting on glass and porcelain almost seven years ago, I never dreamed it would practically take over my life. As I look around my studio, it is crammed full of glass and porcelain pieces just begging to be painted. I have painted so many pieces over the past years that I have lost count. Even today I still manage to paint at least a little bit every day. And to think it all started when I was looking for a way to dress up some champagne flutes for a party!

If you think about it, painting on glass and porcelain doesn't take special skills or lots of special equipment—just paint and some way to apply it. You could even pull your glasses or dishes out of your cabinet right now and get started! Even if you have never picked up a paintbrush before, *you can do this*. It really allows you to easily add color and life to your kitchen, dining room and gifts. It allows you to have fun and be creative in a new way by customizing your own designer patterns and embellishments to your kitchen and entertaining themes.

This book will give you all the tools, tips and inspiration you'll need to get started creating your own masterpieces. In no time you'll start running out of objects to paint, so keep a lookout for interesting surfaces to customize. Thankfully glass and porcelain pieces are relatively inexpensive and quite abundant anywhere. Some of the most overlooked and favorite places of mine happen to be commercial restaurant supply houses, gourmet shops, tag sales or garage sales, outlets, import stores, closeout stores and retail stores. Don't forget to ask friends, family or even neighbors for pieces you can acquire for free. I must warn you, that's how the "collecting disease" starts!

With all of this said there's only one thing left to do: Leave your inhibitions at the door, turn on the answering machine, get comfy, put on some great music and get started!

Carin Heiden Atkins

Chapter 1

The Basics of Paint

I n the past couple of years, nearly every craft or fine art paint company has come out with its own glass and porcelain paint. With over a dozen paints on the market and more slated to come, it can be confusing to decide what paint is the best for your needs. This chapter will provide detailed information about some of the various paints available.

Choosing the Best Paint

The key to a good-looking and long-lasting project is the paint you choose. There are many different factors you have to consider when choosing a particular paint. There are many types of paint: water-based paints, solvent-based paints, air-cure paints and heat-cure paints. Your first question when selecting a paint should be, What is the surface going to be used for? If it is a platter for food, you would want one type of paint; if you are painting your tile kitchen backsplash, you need a different paint. The next question is, Heat cure or air cure? Putting a platter in the oven to heat-cure the paint is very easy; however, heat-cure paint on a tile backsplash would not be an option, so you could go for either a water-based air-cure paint or a solvent-based paint. The next question is, Water-based or solvent-based paint? Water based paints have many advantages including easy cleanup. Solvent-based paints are great for special effects but require more effort for cleanup. Here is a guide for choosing the best paints for your projects.

Water-Based and Water-Cleanup Paints

Water-based and water-cleanup paints have improved over the years, with better formulations, better color choices, easier cleanup and greater durability on more surfaces. While the majority of these paints are water cleanup and nontoxic, they cannot be thinned with water. When you mix water with these paints in any amount, it can affect the adhesion of the paint to a surface, the paint may become less durable or the color or paint consistency may change. When working with any of these paints, it is important to check within the paint brand line for a recommended thinner or diluent, or on the paint label for thinning instructions. Also, make sure to use a dry brush, which can be rinsed in water and blotted before picking up more paint.

The selection of water-based and water-cleanup paints is quite vast. You can apply these paints with a paintbrush, a squeeze bottle, a palette knife, or even from a marker. Here is a roundup of some of the best water-based paints on the market.

Pébéo Porcelaine 150

Water Cleanup / Resin Based / Heat Cure

- 46 translucent and opaque colors
- 4 mediums: gloss, matte, filler undercoat and diluent
- 10 outliners
- 9 markers

Pébéo Porcelaine 150 paint bottles

Porcelaine 150 paint was one of the first heat-cure glass and porcelain paints to hit the market. It was developed to mimic the look of a ceramic glaze when used on porcelain. The paint is meant to hold brush marks, but the look can be softened by using a natural hair paintbrush, color shaper or applicator bottle. The colors are vibrant, beautiful, true colors that are striking on their own or easily mixed to create a customized palette. They also have four brilliant metallics, Gold, Vermeil (red-gold), Copper and Pewter, that are really gorgeous. Porcelaine 150 is thinner than most paints, so it allows you to create a sheer translucent look with one coat, or a thicker opaque look by layering two or three coats. In addition to the paint, you can choose from ten colors of outliners to create raised outlines perfect for personalizing designs, creating a stained glass look or adding texture to any piece. The outliners are great for creating quick and easy projects and getting into tight areas. They are especially good for children who want to paint. This paint does have to be heat-cured in your home oven at 300°F (150°C) for thirty to thirty-five minutes in order for it to be permanent. It comes out of the oven with a gloss

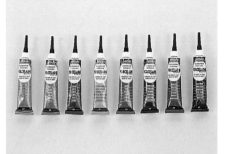
Pébéo Porcelaine 150 Cloisonné Outliners

Pébéo Porcelaine 150 markers

enamel finish. Until it is heat-set, you can wash the paint off with warm water, glass cleaner, or rubbing alcohol.

Delta PermEnamel

Water Cleanup / Polyester Based / Air Cure

- 60 satin colors, including metallics
- 7 frosted colors
- 7 shimmer colors
- 7 mediums: surface conditioner, retarder, glitter glaze, gloss glaze, diluent, satin glaze and metal primer
- 3 outliners in White, Black and Gold

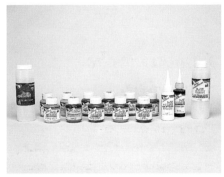
DeltaPermEnamel paint products

Delta PermEnamel paint is the first polyester-based paint introduced for painting on tile, glass and ceramics. It is an air-dry paint that is perfect for painting on any surface that can't be put in the oven for heat-curing. Delta PermEnamel is dishwasher safe and oven safe up to 350° F (175°C) after the surface has been allowed to air-cure for ten days before being washed.

The PermEnamel painting system is a three-step process. First, you must prepare the surface with a specially formulated surface conditioner that contains bonding agents to aid adhesion. Next you are ready to paint your surface with any of the

PermEnamel satin colors, frosted colors or shimmers. Finally, after the paint is dry, you must protect your work with one of the clear glazes. It is very important not to mix or thin PermEnamel with water because it will greatly affect the adhesion and quality of the paint. You can thin the paint with the satin or gloss glazes for a more translucent look. With over seventy-four colors to choose from, I dare you not to find the colors of your dreams to paint with.

Liquitex Glossies
Water Cleanup / Acrylic Based / Heat Cure

- 24 opaque glossy enamel colors, including Gold, Copper and Silver

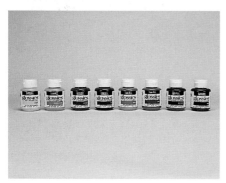

Liquitex Glossies

Liquitex Glossies have been around for many years as great acrylic enamel paints for general use in arts and crafts. Glossies are very smooth paints to apply, gliding onto glass and ceramics easily. Even though the color selection is not as vast as with the other brands, Liquitex Glossies have a great selection to choose from, with beautiful colors to use straight out of the bottle or to mix. To heat-set this paint, use one of

two methods: Bake in a well-ventilated space due to the odor of the fumes at 325°F (160°C) for forty-five minutes, or for pieces too large for the oven, heat-cure them by using a heat gun blowing directly on the surface for thirty minutes. Once the piece is heat-set, the paint will have a glossy, scratch-resistant finish.

Pébéo Vitrea 160 Glass Paint
Water Cleanup / Resin Based / Heat Cure

- 20 glossy colors
- 10 frosted colors
- 9 glossy color markers
- 8 frosted color markers and 1 neutral etching marker
- 6 mediums: diluent, iridescent medium, gloss medium, frosted medium, crackle medium (step 1 and step 2)
- 10 glossy outliners including Pearl White, Gold, and Pewter Metallic

Vitrea 160 paint is a new paint from Pébéo specially formulated for glass. Vitrea 160 allows you to create amazing effects on glass, such as gloss finishes, frosted finishes, crackled finishes, iridescent finishes and even the appearance of body-dyed glass. Even though the paint is formulated for glass, it can also be used on china, enamelware and mirrors. The thirty beautiful colors are easily mixable to create new colors. You can create fabulous looks easily and quickly with the different options this paint provides. The paint has to be baked in your home oven at

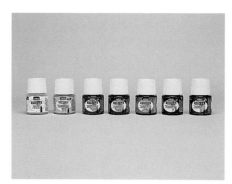

Pébéo Vitrea 160 paint bottles

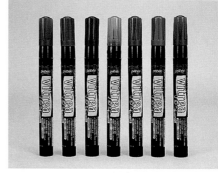

Pébéo Vitrea 160 markers

Pébéo Vitrea 160 outliners

325°F (160°C) for forty minutes to be permanent. Once it is heat-cured it is dishwasher safe. Until the piece is baked, you can remove any mistakes using water, glass cleaner, or rubbing alcohol.

DecoArt Ultra Gloss
Water Cleanup / Acrylic Based / Air or Heat Cure

- 36 opaque colors including metallic, glitter and pearlescent colors
- clear medium

Duncan's Tulip Dimensional Craft and Fabric Paint
Water Based / Acrylic Based / Air Cure

- 40 glossy colors
- 33 pearlescent colors
- 18 matte colors
- 11 glitter colors
- 8 crystal colors
- 6 puffy colors
- 4 glow-in-the-dark colors

While Tulip Dimensional Craft and Fabric Paint is most used for creating wearable art, it can also be used on

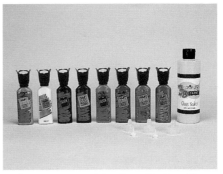

Tulip Dimensional Craft and Fabric Paint

decorative art pieces. The Tulip line has over 120 colors to choose from, and the best feature of this paint is you can apply it to any surface by squeezing it right out of the bottle. If you happen to be afraid of paint-brushes, there is a lot you can accomplish with this paint. It can

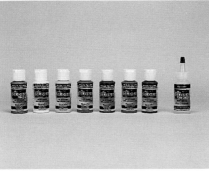

DecoArt Ultra Gloss products

DecoArt Ultra Gloss paint is a new type of acrylic enamel formulated to work without water. It is durable on virtually any hard surface and can be combined with the gloss medium to create soft tints or even glazes. The color palette is beautiful with easy mixing ability. I especially love the pearlescent colors. It is a very smooth paint packed with a lot of pigment. To clean up the paint, use vinegar or rubbing alcohol to degrease the painting surface. This paint can be air-cured for seven to ten days, or if you would like your piece to be dishwasher safe, bake it in your home oven at 325°F (160°C) for thirty minutes. Be careful with pieces coming out of the dishwasher, as the paint tends to be tender or fragile for several hours after washing.

Helpful Hints for Heat-Cure Paint

If you are heat-curing paints in your oven, here are a couple hints to help you achieve great results.

1 **Get an oven thermometer.** It is important to check if your oven is cooking at the proper temperature. If your oven runs hot your paint can burn or scorch. If your oven runs cool, your paint won't cure properly, which could lead to adhesion problems in washing.

2 **Never preheat the oven before heat-curing paint.** You want to warm up the piece and the paint gradually to protect against bubbling.

3 **Never take a piece directly out of the oven after baking.** Crack the oven door open and allow the piece to cool down with the oven. The paint will still be soft; by letting it cool down with the oven you allow the paint to solidify—and your piece won't crack because of a drastic temperature change.

4 **Make sure you have adequate ventilation for paint fumes.** Most of these paints produce mild fumes. It might be helpful to turn on your kitchen exhaust fan or open a window for ventilation if the fumes bother you.

5 **Don't be afraid to heat cure your pieces!** Glass and porcelain can take the heat, they won't melt! It takes most glassware 1300°F to start melting, and porcelain and china more than that, so don't worry!

also be applied with sponges and specialty tips for the Tulip bottles. If you are tired of paints leaving you flat, this is the one to experiment with. Let your piece thoroughly dry (twenty-four to forty-eight hours, depending on the thickness of your paint) before applying a polyurethane sealant.

Pébéo Liquid Crystal
Water Based / Resin Based / Air Cure

- 27 colors
- 4 mediums: anti-UV gloss medium, anti-UV matte medium, crackle medium and anti-adherent

Pébéo Liquid Crystal

Pébéo Liquid Crystal is the air-dry version of Vitrea 160. This thin, color-packed paint is the consistency of a thick watercolor wash. It's great for creating beautiful washes of color on glass. I like to layer different colors on top of each other to create interesting effects. There are also many creative effects you can achieve with the various mediums. This paint works well for tinting and adding bursts of color and can be used with Vitrail Cerne Relief outliners. Liquid Crystal works well on glass, Plexiglas, china, metal and wood. After the paint has air-cured for five days, the paint becomes permanent. This paint is lightfast and

its brilliant color is striking. Some of my favorite surfaces to use this paint on are lightbulbs, glass ornaments and glass bottles.

Pébéo Gel Crystal
Water Based / Resin Based / Air Cure

- 18 crystalline colors
- 10 opaline colors
- 7 iridescents / glitter
- 3 mediums: anti-UV gloss medium, anti-UV matte medium and anti-adherant

Pébéo Gel Crystal is a water-based gel that can add translucent texture to many surfaces including glass, Plexiglas, metal, copper, wood and ceramic. Typically manipulated with a palette knife, Gel Crystal colors can be mixed easily and achieve unique textures other paints can't provide. After forty-eight hours, it dries to a satin finish, depending on the thickness of the gel. Gel Crystal comes in a wide range of color effects, including crystalline, opaline, and iridescent/glitter, to provide you with plenty of design options. With the anti-adherant, you can create shapes, textural stripes or any design that can be peeled off and applied to other pieces. Gel Crystal is extremely lightfast, and with a coat of either the gloss or the matte anti-UV varnish, the vibrant colors will never fade.

Pébéo Gel Crystal products

Solvent-based Paints
Solvent-based paints frighten away many people needlessly. Nightmares of smelly, sticky, permanent paint come to mind, but these fears can be alleviated by using plain old common sense. Solvent-based paints do require more precautions, but the paint effects are well worth it.

When working with solvent-based paints it's important to work in a well-ventilated area. Instead of water, use turpentine, odorless turps, mineral spirits or the new completely safe solvents for cleanup. Working with solvents successfully just requires a few precautions: keep the turpentine and paints covered to limit your exposure; cover your work surface with paper or plastic; wear a smock or painting clothes; and wear latex or plastic gloves.

Pébéo Vitrail
Solvent Based / Resin Based / Air Cure

- 18 transparent colors
- 2 mediums: thinner and varnish
- 10 outliners

Pébéo Vitrail is a brilliant solvent-based paint providing excellent translucency and stunning clear color to any project. My favorite technique with this paint is marbling. Vitrail is easily used on a wide range of surfaces, such as glass, acetate, Plexiglas and metal. The colors are vivid and easily mixable to create a diverse palette. The possibilities are endless for trying and perfecting new painting techniques.

Pébéo Céramic

Solvent Based / Resin Based / Air Cure

- 28 colors including Gold, Silver and Pearl Metallic
- 3 mediums: gloss glaze, filler undercoat and thinner

Pébéo Céramic paint is a brilliant paint for use on ceramic, china, earthenware, stoneware, glass and metal. The twenty-eight beautiful colors are vibrant and easily mixed. You can apply this paint using brushes, sponges, color shapers and marbling techniques. Even without a protective glaze, the paint dries to a stunning high-brilliance finish that is durable enough to withstand scratching. The colors are extremely lightfast and easy to use. For extended durability, seal projects with a clear glaze.

Pébéo Vitrail transparent colors

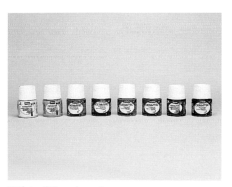

Pébéo Céramic paint

EK Success ZIG Painty Markers

Solvent Based / Paint Markers

- 27 colors in fine and medium tips

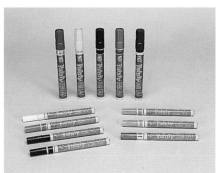

EK Success ZIG Painty markers

Paint markers are easy for anyone to use regardless of one's talent with a paintbrush. I love Painty markers and use them to easily personalize an item or for creative designs on glass, porcelain, ceramics and even plastic. Correct mistakes and clean up with nail polish remover. The colors available are varied and brilliant. These are great all-purpose markers to work with. Paint away without having to use a brush and when you are finished, just wipe the tip to remove any residue, cap tightly and store tip down.

Chapter 2

Painting Tools and Supplies

Next to paint, the major investment in your painting lies in your painting equipment. The quality of your painting tools will determine the quality of the project you produce. In this chapter you will learn about brushes, the basics of brush care, color shapers, applicator bottles, special effects tools and general painting supplies. This will provide a good overview of the tools I have used on projects throughout this book.

Paintbrushes

Paintbrushes are the most important tool in painting and where the majority of your investment lies. In this book I have used both synthetic and natural hair brushes courtesy of Loew-Cornell. It is really important to buy the best brushes you can afford. Synthetic brushes are very versatile in glass and porcelain painting and apply paint well. Natural hair brushes are more expensive and leave fewer brush marks. Natural hair brushes include red sable, squirrel hair or natural hair combinations. Any brush used in glass or porcelain painting must be soft and pliable, not hard and crusty.

Loew-Cornell White Nylon Synthetic Brushes

I like to use white nylon brushes because they are easy to use, are easy to find and hold their shape. These brushes are ideal for beginners and well liked by seasoned painters for their quality and for keeping a good, sharp edge. My recommendation for beginners is to get a good set of brushes, including Series 795 round sizes 2, 3, 5, 6 and 8; Series 801 liner sizes 2 and 4; Series 796 flat shader sizes 6, 8 and 10; and Series 798 flat glaze sizes ½, ¾ and 1. Keep in mind you won't need these all at once! Any of these brushes will get you off to a good start, but it is always good to get the basics and continue adding as you need them.

Loew-Cornell Mixtique Natural Hair Brushes

Mixtique brushes are high-bred brushes incorporating the strength of natural hair (goat, squirrel and red sable) with the durability of synthetic Golden Taklon fiber. What does all that mean? Well, you get the good absorbency and softness of natural hair while getting the strength of synthetic fiber, and the durability needed for glass and porcelain painting. Using this brush or an all natural hair brush will result in fewer brush marks on your pieces, giving your projects a more refined look.

Loew-Cornell white nylon synthetic brushes

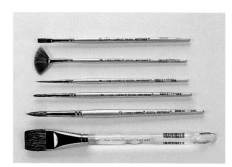

Loew-Cornell Mixtique brushes

Color Shapers

Forsline and Starr Colour Shapers

One of my favorite tools in glass and porcelain painting is the color shaper. I've used Forsline and Starr Colour Shapers throughout this book. If you are not familiar with color shapers, they are used in the fine art world for removing paint and in ceramics as a shaping and carving tool. Made of plastic or rubber, this tool allows you to glide paint right on glass and porcelain easily and effortlessly. The flat chisel makes perfectly even checkerboard designs, along with other great effects. If you have never worked with a color shaper, the technique chapter contains a brief overview of how to use one.

Brush Cleaning and Care

Now that you have invested in your brushes take care of them properly. Good care and good cleaning keep your brushes in optimum condition for your next painting project. When you have new brushes, it is important to break them in. Your brushes will have sizing in the bristles to maintain shape. Rinse your brushes before painting to remove the sizing. After you have finished painting, it is important to rinse your brushes in water or turpentine. If you have used solvent-based paints, use brush cleaner or liquid dish detergent to remove the paint from the bristles and rinse them again. Then using an Ivory soap bar gently scrub the brush into a lather and mold your brushes back into shape with your fingers. When you go to paint next time, simply rinse the brush to remove the soap, which acts as sizing, keeping your brushes in proper form.

As a former brush abuser, I have seen the error of my ways. It has cost me a lot of money to constantly buy new brushes to replace ones I just didn't feel like cleaning or ones I jammed in the water basin while scrubbing the paint out of them. Take it from me: taking good care of your brushes pays off. If your brushes are cared for properly, they will last many years.

Applicator Bottles & Other Accessories

I like to make my painting as easy as possible, and with the help of a few wonderful accessories, I can make any project fun. By far some of my favorite tools are applicator bottles. Pébéo has wonderful applicator bottles, which I use endlessly. They are small plastic bottles with two different metal tips (usually an extra fine and a fine). Each of the metal tips comes with a wire stuck inside it to use as a cleaning tool to keep the metal tip from clogging with paint. Many people discard the wire by mistake, so be sure to hold on to it. The applicator bottles are great for personalizing items, making dots or squiggly lines, laying down outlines and so much more.

In addition Pébéo has other great accessories, including China pencils for drawing a pattern onto a piece, natural hair paintbrushes and applicator sponges. If you are using Tulip Dimensional Craft and Fabric Paint, Duncan makes a package of special effects tips. To use these tips, all you have to do is pop off the built-in applicator tip. (It is best to do this carefully because you can easily squirt paint on yourself.) Once the built-in tip is removed, just pop on or screw on the tip of your choice.

Painting accessories

General Painting Supplies

Here are a few basic supplies you should have on hand while you are painting.

- **A covered work surface.** I like to cover my work surface with craft paper or plastic drop cloths that have been stretched tightly and secured with masking tape.

- **Plenty of soft paper towels or soft cotton rags.** You want to make sure your paper towels or rags are absorbent and soft so you won't damage your brushes or your painting surface.

- **A good water basin.** I like to use Loew-Cornell's brush tub because of its dual basins and brush holders. It acts like three tools in one.

- **Cleaning solutions.** Make sure you have plenty of water, glass cleaner, turpentine or rubbing alcohol.

Applicator Use & Care

When I use applicator bottles, I rarely fill them completely with paint. Instead I fill them only one-third to one-half full. To keep applicator bottles ready for action, make sure to clean them out after use. Running warm water through the bottles cleans them out, and if you have leftover paint residue, swish a little rubbing alcohol in the bottle until it's clean.

Cleaning the metal applicator tips can be difficult but is necessary. Clean metal tips first by using the cleaning wire to remove any paint from the tip. Next, rinse out the tip with warm water until the water runs clear. If there is any leftover residue, fill a small glass jar or plastic margarine tub one-third to one-half full of rubbing alcohol. Close the container and swish the tips around until clean. Don't shake too vigorously as you can break off the tips! I also use this cleaning method when cleaning the Tulip specialty tips.

- **Transfer paper.** You will need this to transfer patterns.

- **Cotton swabs.** These can be used for both cleaning up mistakes and applying paint.

- **Eyedroppers.** Use these for adding paint to the marbling basin or for precise paint mixing.

- **Palette knives.** These are great for applying or manipulating dimensional paint.

- **Latex or plastic gloves.** Use gloves for protection or just to keep your hands clean.

- **Sponges.** Use latex makeup sponges, regular kitchen sponges, scrubby pads and sea sponges to create unique painting effects. My favorites for fine sponging and great coverage are the latex make-up sponges available at your local drugstore.

- **Bamboo skewers or toothpicks.** Use these to engrave in paint, apply paint or scratch away mistakes.

- **Painter's masking tape.** Use masking tape to mask off areas of a surface or to safely secure your paper or plastic to your work surface.

General painting supplies

Painting Techniques

Now that you have learned about the paint, painting tools and supplies, this chapter will show you some basics of painting. This is a general overview of techniques that will be used in projects throughout this book.

Paintbrush Basics

The two types of brushes I work with most are round and flat shader brushes. With these two brushes, I manage to paint just about anything. The strokes I have demonstrated in these photographs are some of the basic strokes I have used throughout the book.

Round Brush Techniques

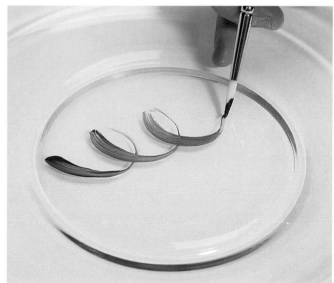

1 To make a comma stroke or pull stroke, load your brush with paint and lightly press your brush on your surface, creating a dot. While releasing the pressure (pull up on the brush), pull the brush down, creating a tail.

2 To make curly lines or streamers, place the brush down and pull to the side, releasing the pressure on the brush. Curve the brush around to create a curlicue.

Flat Brush Techniques

1 Load your brush with paint, making sure there is no paint dripping off the brush. Lightly touch the brush to the surface and pull the brush toward you.

2 In the absence of a taper tip colour shaper, you can make great dots with the end of your paintbrush.

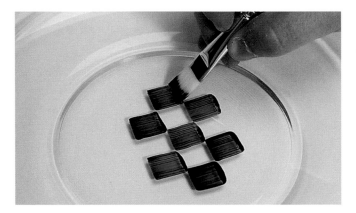

3 To create the perfect checkerboard pattern without having to use a stencil, load your brush with paint and make a top line of squares painted one brush width apart. On the second line, stagger the squares to fill in just below the blank space between the squares on the first line. Repeat this process for the rest of the checkerboard.

4 To make a basketweave pattern, paint diamonds with the brushstroke facing in only one direction. Usually the top line begins with the brush marks facing up. On the second line, the diamond brush marks should face down.

Painting With Color Shapers

While color shapers are widely used in the painting world to remove paint, I tend to do just the opposite. I use these rubber-tipped implements to apply paint. The paint just slides right off to give you an easy brushstroke-free look. There are three different color shapers I use on a regular basis: a flat chisel, a pointed taper tip and an angled chisel tip. I use the flat chisel color shapers for making the perfect checkerboard, diamonds or stripes. I use the pointed taper tip for making even dots, comma strokes and ribbon strokes. I continue to experiment with the angled chisel tip to make great curly lines, streamers, even an abstract basketweave pattern. I encourage you to experiment with these tools and discover your own trademark strokes.

Color Shaper Techniques

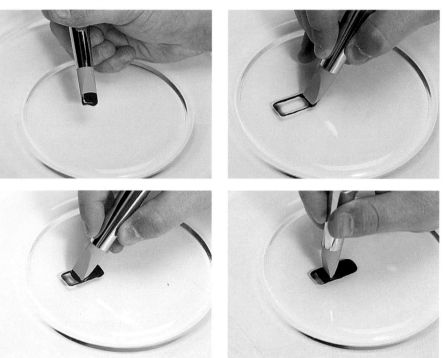

1 Using a flat chisel color shaper, dip shaper in paint on one side of the chisel tip. Draw the color shaper a short distance across the surface, making the edges of the line. Keeping the color shaper at the same angle, push the colour shaper back. This motion will fill in the spaces between the lines. Tap color into areas left unfilled.

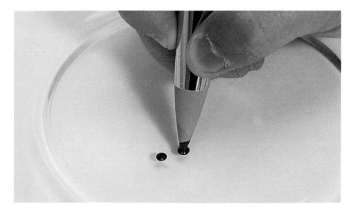

2 Use the taper tip color shaper to make perfect symmetrical dots.

3 You can also use the taper tip to make streamers or ribbons.

Projects

Now that you've learned the painting basics, you are ready to create beautiful designs on porcelain and glass that will enhance any dining room table.

Be on the lookout for the helpful rating boxes at the beginning of each project that tell you the relative ease of each project, the approximate total cost of materials and the time needed to complete the project. Then let your own creative spirit take over and have fun painting these delightful projects!

Explanation of Symbols

Difficulty
• Difficulty is rated on a scale of one to five; 1 is easy, 5 is difficult

= easy

= difficult

Cost
• $1 to 25 = $
• $25 to 50 = $$
• $50 to 75 = $$$
• $75 to 100 = $$$$
• $100 to 125 = $$$$$

Time
• Projects range from 15 minutes to 4 hours
• None of the times include drying time or heat-curing time

= 15 minutes

= 1 hour

Cheery Cherry Platter

Designed to make you smile whenever you use it, the Cheery

Cherry Platter is easy for anyone to complete in under an hour.

The vibrant reds of the cherries and the vivid yellow scrolls make

this platter a whimsical yet elegant addition to any decor.

Materials

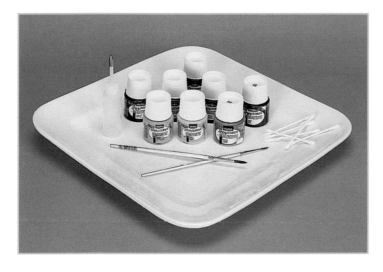

Pébéo Porcelaine 150
- Anthracite (42)
- Bronze (28)
- Citrine (01)
- Etruscan Red (12)
- Malachite (26)
- Marseille Yellow (02)
- Ruby (07)
- Tourmaline (10)

Loew-Cornell Mixtique Brushes
- Series 8000 no. 3 round
- Series 8000 no. 6 round

- ceramic whiteware platter
- 1 package Pébéo Applicator Bottles
- cherry pattern (page 117)
- transfer paper
- glass cleaner or rubbing alcohol
- paper towels or soft cotton rags
- cotton swabs
- pencil or stylus

Difficulty: 🖌🖌

Cost: $$

Time: 🕐

1 Clean painting surface

Wipe surface thoroughly with glass cleaner or rubbing alcohol to degrease your platter. Be careful to avoid transferring hand oils to the paint surface.

2 Transfer cherry pattern

Place transfer paper on the platter where you want to place a cherry cluster, making sure the transfer pattern is face down. Lay the cherry pattern from page 117 over the transfer paper and trace with a pencil or stylus. Repeat around the border of the platter, spacing cherries about 3" (8cm) apart (this may vary with your platter).

3 Basecoat cherries

Basecoat the middle of each side of the cherries with Ruby and a no. 6 round brush, almost creating the look of parentheses.

Hint

To create a more whimsical-looking platter, try alternating the way your cherry clusters face. For instance, on my platter, some of the cherry clusters are a little higher or lower than the clusters sitting next to them. Some of the clusters face to the right, to the left or even straight. Mix it up! It will add your own personal touch to your piece.

4 Shade cherries

Shade the inside top of the cherries with Tourmaline and a no. 3 round brush.

5 Paint contours

Contour the outside of each cherry with Etruscan Red and a no. 3 round brush, rounding out the look of your cherries.

6 Basecoat leaves

Basecoat leaves with Bronze and a no. 6 round brush to create the background color for the leaves.

7 Highlight leaves

Highlight in the middle of each leaf with Malachite using a no. 3 round brush. Allow this to dry for ten minutes before continuing to the next step.

8 Create details and outlines

Pour Anthracite into an applicator, filling it only one-third to one-half full, and attach a metal tip. Use the applicator bottle to outline the cherries and leaves and to draw in the vein detail on the leaves and cherry cluster stems. When drawing in the stems you don't have to be perfect. Be a bit sketchy in your line details.

9 Paint scrolls

Paint scrolls in between the cherry clusters with Citrine and your no. 6 round brush.

10 Shade scrolls

Shade the scrolls where needed for contrast with Marseille Yellow and a no. 3 round brush.

11 Heat-cure finished platter

Use the cotton swabs to clean up any mistakes. Allow your completed platter to air-dry according to the paint label instructions, then place it in a cold oven. After placing your platter in the oven, turn it on to 300°F (150°C) for thirty to thirty-five minutes. When the baking process is complete, crack the door open and allow the platter to cool with the oven for approximately twenty to thirty minutes.

This is the perfect opportunity to make over your plain wine glasses or even water goblets! Any beautifully shaped goblet or glass will work wonderfully for this project. These rose glasses are perfect for livening up your table, or they can be used as a creative votive candle holders.

Materials

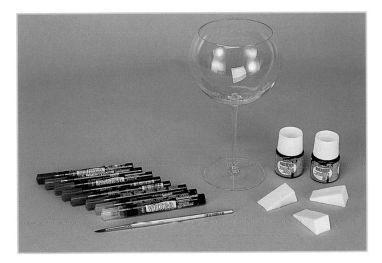

Pébéo Vitrea 160
- Oriental Green (13) (gloss)
- Aniseed (38) (frost)
- Iridescent Medium

Pébéo Vitrea 160 Markers
- Pink (frost)
- Pink (gloss)
- Red (gloss)
- Dark Green (gloss)

Loew-Cornell Mixtique Brush
- no. 6 round

- 2 bordeaux wine goblets (10–12 oz)
- latex makeup sponges
- glass cleaner or rubbing alcohol
- paper towels or soft cotton rags

Difficulty:

Cost: **$$**

Time:

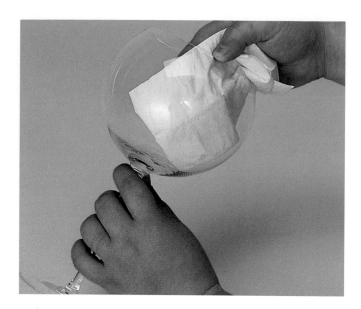

1 Clean painting surface

Wipe the surface thoroughly with glass cleaner or rubbing alcohol to degrease the goblet and help the paint adhere.

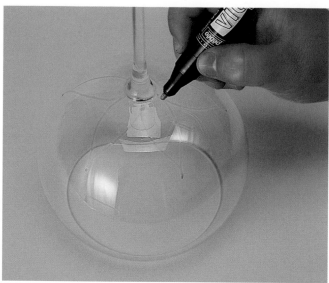

2 Draw sepals

Using the Dark Green marker, draw in the sepals on the underside of the goblet bowl.

Hint

Priming Paint Markers

Starting a new marker can sometimes try your patience! This process is called priming. To prime your paint markers, shake the marker with the cap on for about ten seconds. Remove the cap and press down on the felt and release. Set the marker tip down on a piece of paper towel and lean it up against something. By the force of gravity the paint will come down into the felt tip. If it does not work the first time you can repeat the process again. The important thing to remember: do not continuously press up and down on the felt. Two things are likely to happen; first you will damage the felt tip, and second you might cause the paint to explode out of the tip leaving you with a big mess. When you have completed your use of the markers wipe the tips of your markers to remove any surface residue, then cap tightly and store horizontally or tip down.

3 Paint base of goblet

Sponge Oriental Green over the base of the goblet using a makeup sponge. You may choose to add hints of Aniseed to achieve a more natural or variegated look.

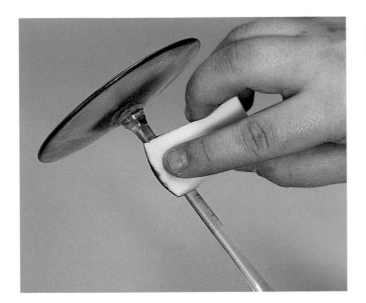

Hint

Removing Mistakes

To remove mistakes on the goblet use cotton swabs lightly dampened with glass cleaner or rubbing alcohol. It's important to smooth any stray fibers to keep from removing areas you really want to keep.

To remove larger areas I use a latex sponge dampened with Windex or rubbing alcohol. This will enable you to remove large areas of paint quickly. When removing large areas of paint that have been on the surface for a while, it may take a little elbow grease. For those cases I use a kitchen sponge to remove the paint.

4 Paint stem

Sponge Oriental Green over the stem of the goblet.

5 Paint in sepals

Paint in the sepals with Oriental Green and a no. 6 round brush.

6 Draw rose petals

Draw in rose petals with the Pink frost marker. Start forming your petals at the bottom and position in rows. The rows of petals should alternate, filling in the gaps of the row before.

7 Fill in petals

Fill in about ¼" (6mm) under the outline of the petals with the frosted Pink marker to make the curled over edge of the petals.

8 Fill in shading

Fill in shading at the base of each petal with the glossy Red marker.

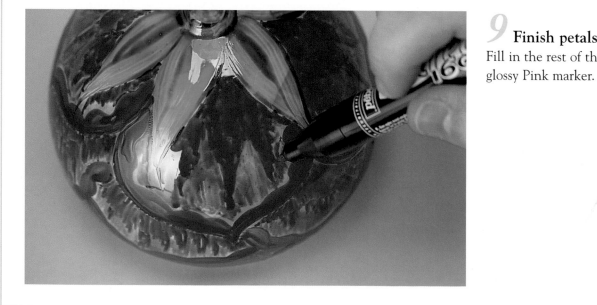

9 Finish petals

Fill in the rest of the petal with the glossy Pink marker.

10 Add iridescent medium

To add interest, paint iridescent medium over the glossy part of the petal, avoiding the frosted top edge of the petal. Apply iridescent medium with no. 6 round brush.

11 Heat-cure paint

Allow goblet to air-dry per paint label instructions then heat cure in home oven at 325°F (160°C) for forty minutes.

Start your day in a beautiful way by drinking your morning tea

from this elegant all-in-one teapot. Treat yourself to a piece of luxury

by easily making this for yourself or as a gift—in only one afternoon.

Materials

DecoArt Ultra Gloss
- Cadmium Yellow (DG06)
- Emerald Pearl (DG63)
- Gloss White(DG01)
- Golden Pearl (DG65)
- Hunter (DG12)
- Sage Green (DG57)

Loew-Cornell White Nylon Brushes
- Series 795 no. 5 round
- Series 796 no. 10 flat shader

- all-in-one teapot
- latex makeup sponges
- paper towels or soft cotton rags
- vinegar, rubbing alcohol or glass cleaner

Difficulty:

Cost: **$$**

Time: ⏱

1 Clean painting surface

Thoroughly clean the painting surface with glass cleaner, vinegar or rubbing alcohol.

2 Paint gold accents

Paint the lid, spout, teapot handle, cup handle and cup base in Golden Pearl with a no. 10 flat brush.

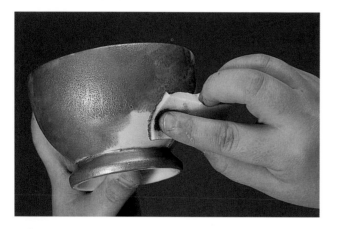

Pieces with completed basecoat

3 Paint basecoat

Using a latex sponge, sponge paint Emerald Pearl over the body of the cup and teapot, making sure to avoid the gold areas.

4 Paint daisies

Paint small daisies in groups of three in a random pattern all over the green areas of the cup and teapot. To make daisies, use Gloss White and a no. 5 round brush. Press your brush down, making a large dot, then lift the brush so only the tip of the brush is on the surface and pull the brush into the center of the flower.

5 Paint daisy centers

Dip the end of your paintbrush in Cadmium Yellow. Use this to make a yellow dot in the center of each flower.

6 Paint leaves

Use Hunter Green and your no. 5 round brush to pull short strokes around the flower groupings to suggest leaves.

7 Highlight leaves

Highlight each leaf with a smaller stroke of Sage Green.

8 Paint accents and cure paint

To finish the piece, make bands of Hunter around the tip of the spout, the handles and the top of the teacup base. Allow the finished piece to air-cure for seven days or heat-cure in your home oven at 325°F (160°C) for thirty minutes.

Marbled Plates

Make your own one-of-a-kind plates in minutes. If you want to make

a stunning impression at your next dinner party, these plates are sure to

catch everyone's eye. With the help of solvent-based paints that float

on water, it has never been easier to achieve a marbled look on glass.

Once you do one plate you'll be hooked!

Materials

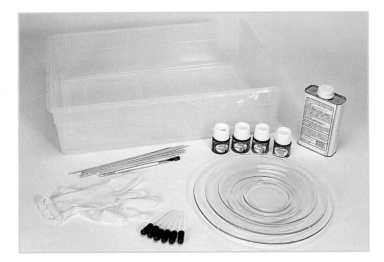

Pébéo Vitrail
- Crimson (12)
- Purple (26)
- Rose Pink (21)
- Turquoise Blue (17)

Loew-Cornell Mixtique brush
- Series 8300 no. 6 flat shader brush

- glass plates for 4 place settings
  (a setting includes salad plate, dinner plate
  and service charger plate)
- eyedroppers
- gloss varnish
- latex or plastic gloves
- bamboo skewers
- plastic tub (I used a 6" [15 cm] deep tub,
  22" x 16" [56 cm x 41 cm])
- turpentine
- paper towels or soft cotton rags
- glass cleaner

Difficulty:

Cost: $$

Time: !

1 Clean painting surface

Thoroughly clean both sides of each plate with glass cleaner.

2 Paint band

Use a no. 6 flat shader brush to paint a band of Turquoise Blue around the edge of the bottom side of the plate. The band should be the same width as your brush. Immediately after completing your plate, carefully clean your brush with turpentine.

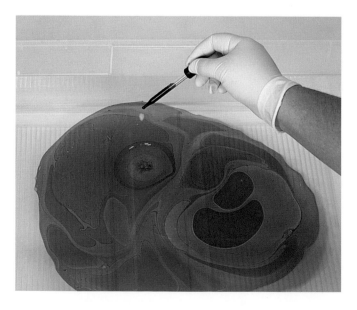

3 Add paint to water

Fill a plastic tub with water. Use separate eyedroppers to randomly dot the surface of the water with Crimson, Purple, and Rose Pink.

4 Create marble pattern

Swirl the paint around to create a marble pattern. If you don't like your pattern, simply drag your bamboo skewer through, swirling it around to collect all of the paint into a ball at the end of the skewer.

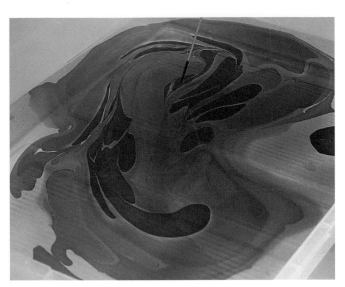

Completed pattern ready for dipping

5 Dip plate

Wearing latex or plastic gloves, carefully hold the plate by the very edges and dip it into the water basin at a slight angle, allowing the paint film on the surface of the water to cover the underside of the plate.

6 Allow paint to dry

After the film attaches to the plate, carefully lift the plate out of the basin, setting it paint side up on a work surface to dry.

7 Create speckled pattern

To create a more mottled effect, place the tip of the dropper just below the surface of the water. Squeeze the eyedropper to release bubbles of paint and air to create a speckled pattern.

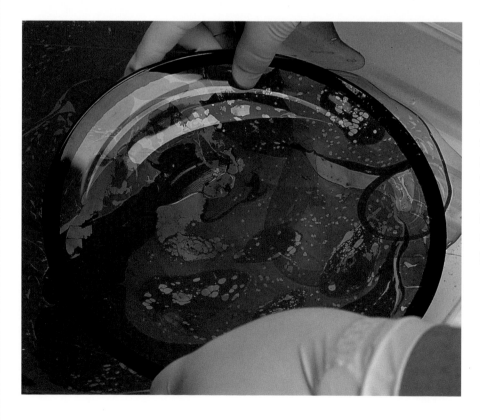

8 Create complex marbling

To create a more complex marbling pattern, you can redip the plate in the basin. The first layer of marbling will not come off during subsequent dippings. Once you have finished marbelizing, it is important to clean your basin and eyedroppers quickly. Empty the basin and use turpentine and paper towels to remove any residual paint. Clean the eyedroppers with turpentine.

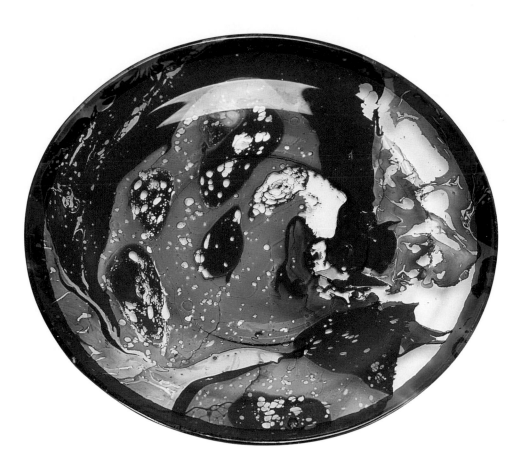

9 Finish plates

Allow the plates to dry completely. This can be aided with a hair dryer. Next, seal the plates with a gloss varnish. To store the plates, place a sheet of waxed paper between each plate to ensure the plates do not stick. Hand washing is recommended.

Party Time Cake Plate and Dome

Have a party every day. This festive cake plate and dome
give an air of celebration to any ordinary day. The colorful
streamers and jovial party faces are a colorful boost
to any decor and add a special touch to sweet treats.

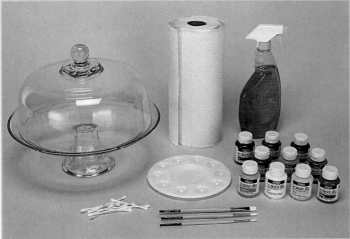

Materials

Liquitex Glossies
- Almond
- Black
- Blue
- Green
- Magenta
- Pink
- Red
- Red Purple
- White
- Yellow
- Yellow Orange
- Any other colors you choose

Loew-Cornell White Nylon Brushes
- Series 795 no. 3 round
- Series 795 no. 6 round
- Series 796 no. 10 flat shader

- glass cake dome
- cotton swabs
- toothpicks or bamboo skewers
- plastic paint palette
- glass cleaner or rubbing alcohol
- paper towels or soft cotton rags

Difficulty:

Cost: $$$

Time:

1 Clean painting surface

Thoroughly clean entire surface with glass cleaner or rubbing alcohol.

2 Paint stripes

Paint stripes on the underside of the pedestal plate with Red Purple and a no. 10 flat shader brush, spacing the stripes one brush width apart.

3 Paint dots

Add white dots between stripes. Dip the end of your paintbrush in White paint and make a line of four dots between each Red Purple stripe.

4 Paint streamers

Use your no. 6 round brush to paint curly streamers on the underside of the pedestal plate with Red, Blue, Yellow, Green and Magenta.

5 Add white dots to streamers

Intersperse white dots among the streamers using the end of your brush.

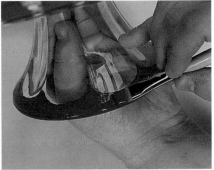

6 Paint border on pedestal base

Paint Red Purple on the pedestal base. Use the no. 10 flat shader brush to paint the bottom edge of the pedestal base. Follow the contours of the pedestal as a guide.

7 Highlight border

Add a White border at the top of the Red Purple border with your no. 3 round brush.

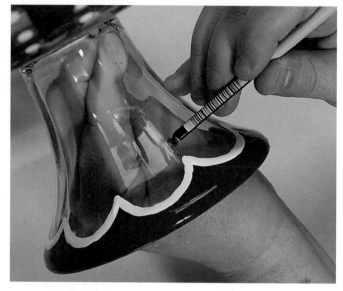

8 Add green dots

Using the end of your brush, paint Green dots on the pedestal at the top of each peak of the border.

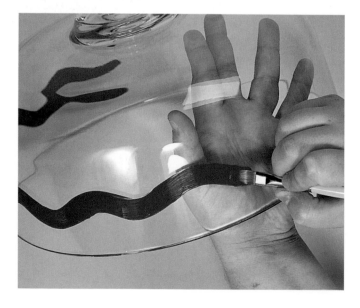

9 Paint wavy border on cake dome

Using your no. 10 flat shader brush and Red Purple, paint a wide, wavy border about 1½"to 2" (4cm to 5cm) from the edge of the cake dome.

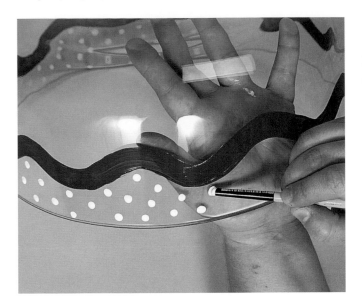

10 Add white dots

Fill in the space under the border with random White dots made with the end of your paintbrush.

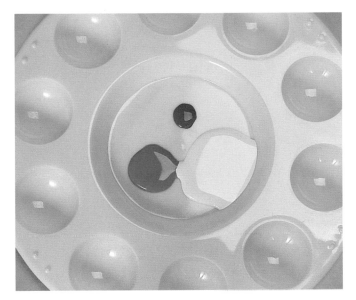

11 Mix colors for skin tones

To mix peach flesh tones for faces, squeeze out a 1½" (4 cm) puddle of White, 1" (3cm) puddle of Yellow Orange and a little under ¾" (2cm) puddle of Pink and stir together with your brush. Use Almond for brown skin tones.

12 Basecoat faces

Dip the tip of your finger in one skin tone and make a small circular motion with your finger to form a face. Dab the circle to fill in color.

13 Basecoat hats

Using your no. 3 round brush, basecoat hats in a triangle shape in a selection of colors.

14 Add streamers

Paint curly streamers in Pink, Red, Green, Yellow, Blue and Yellow Orange.

15 Detail party hats

Paint designs in various colors on the hats. I also added pompons and streamers to the party hats.

16 Add facial features

Use Black paint and a toothpick or bamboo skewer to lightly dab on eyes and apply smiles on the basecoated faces.

17 Paint dome knob

Using the no. 10 flat shader brush, cover the entire knob with Red Purple. You might need two coats to get opaque coverage.

18 Add white dots

Use the end of your brush to make White dots around the base of the knob.

19 Heat-cure paint

To finish the cake plate and dome, make sure to fix any mistakes before the baking process, either with a cotton swab moistened with glass cleaner or with a razor blade when the paint is dry. When you are finished, let the piece air-dry before placing it in a cool oven. Turn the oven to 325°F (160°C) for thirty to thirty-five minutes. Make sure your kitchen is well ventilated during the baking process because this paint does produce fumes. Allow the piece to cool with the oven after baking.

Variations

A great way to continue the celebration theme is to paint complementary plates and goblets. Add a festive ice bucket for a complete set of party glassware.

Flying Butterfly Soup Tureen

What a way to dress up your soups and stews! This lively soup tureen

is perfect for all-season use; it is particularly delightful during the

dark days of winter to remind you spring is not far away.

Materials

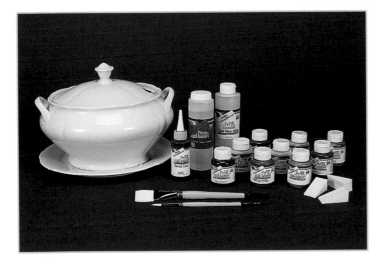

Delta PermEnamel
- Beyond Turquoise
- Cape Cod Blue
- Country Tomato
- Crocus Yellow
- Deep Coral
- Fire Red
- Light Burgundy
- Lilac Lace
- Royal Blue
- Tangerine
- Ultra Black
- Ultra White

Loew-Cornell White Nylon Brushes
- Series 798 ¾" (19 mm) flat glaze/wash
- Series 795 no. 5 round
- Series 796 no. 8 flat shader

- Delta PermEnamel Black Accent Liner
- Delta PermEnamel Gloss Glaze
- Delta PermEnamel Surface Conditioner
- white porcelain soup tureen
- butterfly pattern (page 116)
- transfer paper
- latex makeup sponges
- paper towels or soft cotton rags

Difficulty:

Cost: **$$**

Time:

1 Clean painting surface

Use plain water to wipe the painting surface clean.

2 Apply Surface Conditioner

Using Surface Conditioner, condition all painting surfaces. After applying, allow to dry. Do not wipe off.

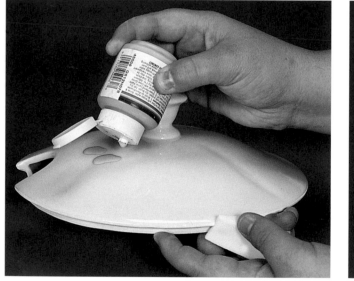

3 Apply basecoat

Add Cape Cod Blue directly to surface.

Hint

It is very important to use PermEnamel Surface Conditioner rather than glass cleaner or rubbing alcohol to clean your painting surface for this project. Surface Conditioner has special bonding agents that aid in the adhesion of PermEnamel paint to the surface and provide stronger paint durability.

4 Sponge paint entire surface

Using a latex makeup sponge, dab the Cape Code Blue all over to completely cover surface. Repeat this for all the pieces and allow them to dry.

5 Sponge paint clouds

Use a clean latex makeup sponge to create white clouds with Ultra White.

6 Add highlights to clouds

Use your finger to apply bright white cloud highlights.

7 Complete sky background

Add clouds to all the pieces to complete the background.

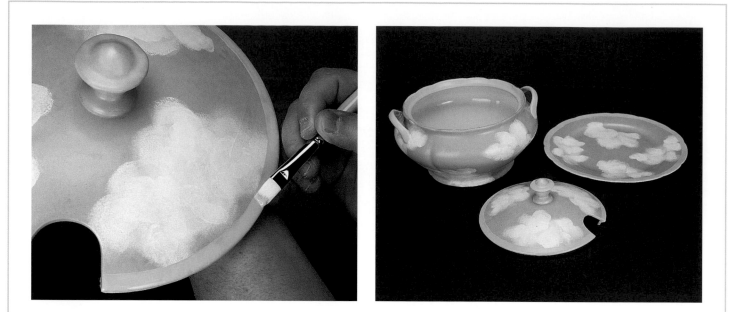

8 Paint border

Using a no. 8 flat shader brush, paint a band of Crocus Yellow around the edge of the lid, around the top of the tureen, on the handles, on the lid pull and around the platter rim. The band should be a brush width wide.

Hint

When painting with PermEnamel, it is very important to work with a dry brush. It is OK to rinse your brush with water, but be sure to remove as much moisture as possible from your brush before picking up more paint.

9 Draw butterfly bodies

Place the transfer paper on the lid where you want to place a butterfly, making sure the transfer pattern is face down. Lay the butterfly pattern from page 116 over the transfer paper and trace with a pencil or stylus. Allow ample room for wings. Fill in the heads and bodies of the butterflies with the Black Accent Liner.

10 Basecoat wings

Basecoat all butterfly wings in Ultra White.

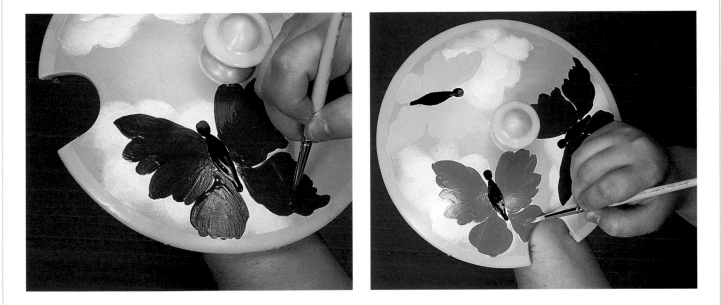

11 Paint butterflies

Using your no. 5 round brush, paint over the white basecoated butterflies with the colors of your choice. In this example, I have used Country Tomato, Beyond Turquoise and Crocus Yellow.

12 Shade in wings

Using a no. 5 round brush, shade inside the wings with a darker color than the basecoat. Leave a border of the basecoat visible (approximately ¼" to ½" [6mm to 13mm]). In this case, I used Light Burgundy for shading the red butterfly.

13 Add highlights

Add a highlight of lighter color on top of the darker shade, again leaving a border of darker color visible. In this example, I used Fire Red as a highlight.

14 Paint dots

Using the end of your paint brush, add contrasting dots of Ultra White and Crocus Yellow to the wings.

15 Outline wings

Using the Accent Liner, outline the butterfly wings in Black, making the separation between the upper and lower wings.

16 Paint antennae

Using Ultra Black and your no. 5 round brush, add curly antennae. Finish all of the butterflies following steps 11–16 on all pieces. For the yellow butterfly use Crocus Yellow (step 11), Tangerine (step 12), Deep Coral (step 13) and Ultra White (step 14). For the blue butterfly use Beyond Turquoise (step 11), Royal Blue (step 12), Lilac Lace (step 13) and Ultra White (step 14).

17 Detail lid pull

Detail the lid pull with your no. 5 round brush by painting it Fire Red with a Crocus Yellow border.

18 Add accent dots and glaze

Using the Accent Liner, detail the lid pull with little black dots around the top. When the paint is dry, use a ¾" (19mm) wash brush to coat all the painted surfaces with Gloss Glaze.

19 Air-cure paint

Complete the tureen by applying a coat of Gloss Glaze with the glaze/wash brush. Allow the completed tureen to air-cure for ten days before you use or wash it. After curing, this piece is dishwasher and microwave safe.

Completed soup tureen lid

Completed base plate

Completed soup basin

Variations

Using Pébéo Porcelaine 150 paint, here's another way to use the butterfly motif to create colorful, garden-inspired pieces covered in lush flowers.

Celebration Champagne Flutes

Perfect for a special toast, these champagne flutes echo a richly toned autumn color scheme. Elegantly detailed with gold accents, these glasses will sparkle when filled with your favorite champagne, turning an ordinary event into an unforgettable celebration.

Materials

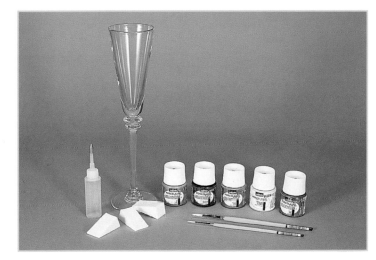

Pébéo Porcelaine 150
- Copper (46)
- Etruscan Red (12)
- Gold (44)
- Vermeil (45)
- Matte Medium

Loew-Cornell White Nylon Brushes
- Series 795 no. 3 round
- Series 795 no. 6 round

- 2 champagne flutes
- leaf pattern (page 117)
- 1 package Pébéo Applicator Bottles
- latex makeup sponges
- glass cleaner or rubbing alcohol

Difficulty:

Cost: $$

Time: !

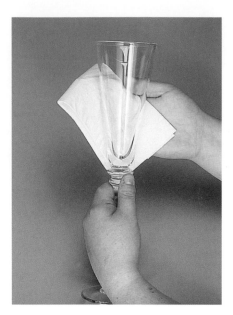

1 Clean painting surface

Thoroughly clean surface with glass cleaner or rubbing alcohol.

Hint

It is very important to completely stir up the Porcelaine 150 metallic colors. Because the pigment is so heavy, it tends to settle in the bottom of the jar during shipping. Use the end of your paintbrush to stir the paint. It should be a rich, smooth metallic mixture after stirring completely. I tend to stir really well and then shake; however, be careful not to shake too vigorously because shaking can produce air bubbles in the paint.

2 Basecoat leaves

Use a no. 5 round brush to basecoat the three leaves encircling the flute with Gold. Using the leaf pattern on page 117 as a guide, draw a wavy line for the center vein. Fill in by pulling strokes from the edge toward the center, keeping a serrated edge.

3 Fill in leaves

Leaving a border of the gold, use a no. 3 round brush to fill in the center of the leaves with Vermeil.

4 Fill in leaf center

Leaving a border of Vermeil, fill in the centers of the leaves with Copper.

5 Outline leaves

Fill an applicator bottle no more than half full with Gold and attach the finer of the two metal applicator tips. Use the paint to sketchily outline around the edges of the leaves and along the central vein. Add a few suggestions of interior veins as well.

6 Paint swirl design

With a no. 3 round brush and matte medium, paint a loose swirl starting near the top of the glass between two leaves. End the swirl where the leaves join or overlap.

7 Add dots

Dip the end of your brush in Etruscan Red and apply a dot between each swirl.

8 Paint disks

Using your no. 3 round brush, paint the disks above the stem with Etruscan Red.

9 Sponge paint stem

Use a latex makeup sponge to sponge matte medium evenly over the stem of the flute.

10 Sponge paint base

Sponge Etruscan Red on the underside of the base of the flute. You may need two coats for good coverage. Be careful not to set the flute down right side up! Consider the paint to be wet until it has been baked. For the rest of the steps, hold the flute carefully or set it upside down on its rim.

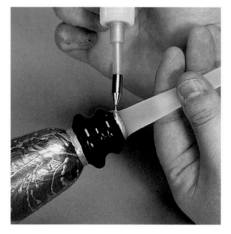

11 Apply gold accents

Use the applicator bottle to apply a thin gold band just below the Etruscan Red disks on the flute stem. Echo the same look at the bottom of the flute stem.

12 Paint matte swirls

Using your no. 3 round brush, paint matte medium swirls around the top side of the base of the flute.

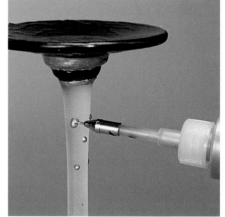

13 Apply gold dots to stem

Set the flute down on its rim and apply small dots of Gold on the stem with the applicator bottle. If the dots begin to run, invert the glass (but don't set it down!) until the dots stop running and begin to set, then return it to its inverted position.

14 Cure paint

Allow your piece to air-dry for twenty-four hours before baking. After the paint has dried, put the piece into a cold oven. Turn the oven on to 300°F (150°C) and bake for thirty minutes. Allow the piece to cool with the oven. Once it has cooled, the piece is dishwasher safe, microwave save and safe for food contact.

Variations

Want an easy way to update or add elegance to a place setting? Using the same patterns on the champagne flute, apply the Gold swirls, Vermeil starbust pattern and rubbed Copper to different areas of various plates with Pébéo Porcelaine 150 Outliners.

Lover's Teapot

This lovely little teapot will inspire you to drink a lot more tea!

Full of whimsy and delight, this teapot is perfect for any occasion,

especially for Valentine's Day breakfast or as a special wedding present.

Materials

Pébéo Porcelaine 150
- Anthracite (42)
- Bronze (28)
- Etruscan Red (12)
- Fuschia (09)
- Gold (44)
- Parma (14)
- Tourmaline (10)

Loew-Cornell White Nylon Brush
- Series 795 no. 3 round brush

Forsline and Starr Colour Shaper
- no. 6 flat chisel
- no. 6 taper tip

- white porcelain teapot
- 1 package Pébéo Applicator Bottles
- glass cleaner or rubbing alcohol
- paper towels or soft cotton rags

Difficulty:

Cost: $$

Time:

1 Clean painting surface

Thoroughly clean surface with glass cleaner or rubbing alcohol.

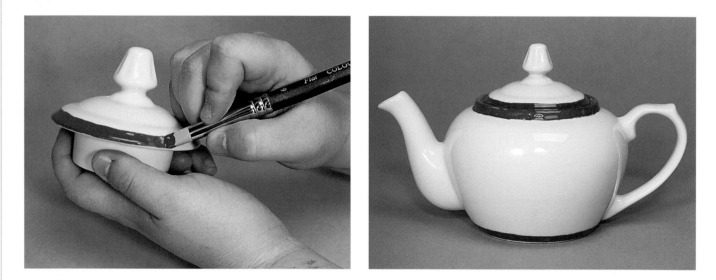

2 Paint border

Use your no. 6 flat chisel color shaper to paint a band of Fuschia along the edge of the teapot lid, the opening of the teapot and the bottom of the teapot. (See techniques chapter on page 19 for tips on working with color shapers.)

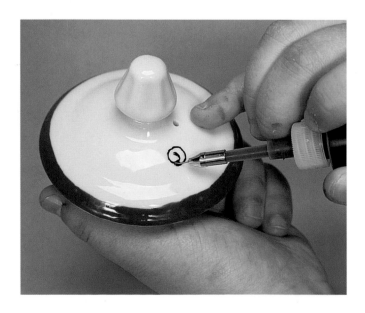

3 Start floral bouquet

Start your floral bouquet with one single flower. Fill your applicator bottle half full with Anthracite and add on one of the metal tips. Outline a spiral, closing it up at one end.

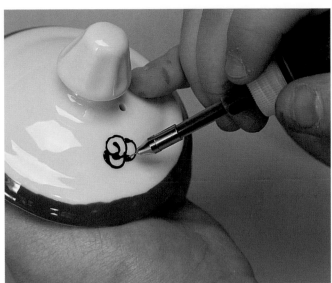

4 Draw semicircle

Draw a semicircle with the applicator bottle along the bottom on one side of the spiral.

5 Complete flower

Repeat step 4 on the other side. Your flower is complete!

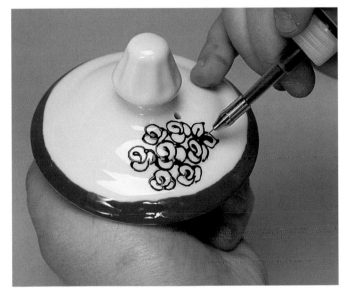

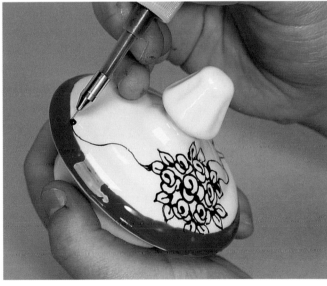

6 Create bouquet

Encircle your original flower with six more flowers, creating a circular bouquet. Add a few leaves between some of the roses on the outer edges.

7 Paint ribbons

Use the applicator bottle to make a streamer or ribbon on either side of the bouquet by first making a wavy line.

8 Draw half circle

Draw a half circle under the original line meeting up with the original line toward the middle.

9 Finish banner

Finish banner by drawing up ¼" (6mm) then left, mimicking the original line. Complete by making a V-cut in the ribbon.

10 Fill in ribbon

Fill in the ribbon with Parma and a no. 3 round brush.

11 Fill in flowers

Fill in the flowers using a small taper tip color shaper with Fuschia, Tourmaline and Etruscan Red.

12 Fill in leaves

Use the taper tip color shaper to fill in the leaves with Bronze.

13 Repeat bouquet

Your finished bouquet should look like this. Repeat it on the lid and on the teapot, being careful to leave room for the gold hearts.

14 Begin heart

To make a heart, start by drawing a backward S-shape with Gold and your color shaper.

15 Complete heart

Mirror your first stroke with a partial forward S on the other side.

16 Paint dots

To complete your heart, place five dots of Gold over the upper right side of the heart. Add more Gold dots on the teapot handle and spout. Repeat steps 14–16 to place hearts around the bouquets on your teapot.

17 Heat-cure paint

Once your teapot is finished allow it to air-dry per paint label instructions. Once it is dry, place it in a cold oven. Turn the oven on to 300°F (150°C) to heat-cure for thirty minutes. Allow the piece to cool with the oven. Once it is heat-cured the teapot is dishwasher safe, microwave safe and safe for food contact.

Variations

Once you have completed your teapot, add complementary teacups and saucers featuring the same ribbon bouquet. Complete the tea set with a sugar bowl using the same technique.

$\mathcal{R}$ainbow Service Charger

These brilliantly colorful service charger plates are an excellent way to dress up your china for special events. Not used for direct food contact, service chargers are used as additional ornamentation to your table. Perfect for beginners, this project uses cotton swabs and a color shaper as paint applicators instead of brushes.

Materials

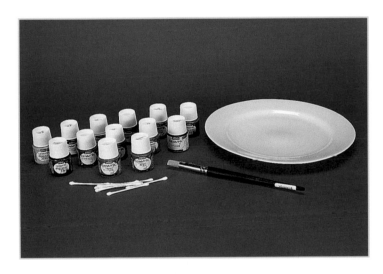

Pébéo Céramic
- Cherry Red (24)
- Garnet Red (20)
- Green (37)
- Lavender (11)
- Leaf Green (27)
- Light Yellow (33)
- Mauve (12)
- Orange (23)
- Orange Yellow (22)
- Rich Gold (15)
- Ruby (29)
- Sevres Blue (25)
- Gloss Glaze

Forsline and Starr Colour Shaper
- no. 6 flat chisel

- 4 white porcelain service chargers (approximately 12" [30 cm] in diameter)
- box of cotton swabs
- latex or plastic gloves
- glass cleaner
- turpentine
- paper towels

Difficulty:

Cost: **$$$$**

Time: ⏳ ⏳ ⏳ ⏳

1 Clean painting surface

Thoroughly clean surface with glass cleaner.

Hint

Working With Solvent-Based Paint

When you use solvent-based paint, it is always a good idea to take a few simple precautions. Completely cover your work surface to avoid paint damage and allow for an easier cleanup. Wear latex or plastic gloves to protect your hands and painting clothes or a smock to protect your clothing. Although Pébéo Céramic paint has very light fumes compared to most solvent-based paints, if fumes easily affect you, a simple dust mask will help. When paints are not in use, put the caps back on them to limit fume exposure. For this project, you won't need to use the turpentine for any great length of time, so keep it capped or covered to avoid unnecessary contact. The turpentine will be used to clean up any mistakes or for cleaning up after the project.

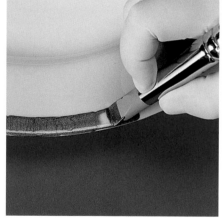

2 Paint gold border

Use a no. 6 flat chisel color shaper to paint a band of Rich Gold around the edge of the charger. Dip the colour shaper in paint, touch the tip to the surface and pull a short stroke. This will create the edges of your border stripe.

3 Fill in

Keeping your color shaper on the same angle, push it back along the path of the stroke. This motion fills in the paint between the edges created in the first step.

4 Tap paint

If the stripe does not fill completely, tap paint into the empty area with the color shaper.

5 Begin pattern

The pattern for the charger is based on an abstract swirl. I started with Light Yellow, dipping a cotton swab into the paint and then dotting or stippling it into my desired pattern.

Hint

Before painting with the cotton swabs, it's important to compact all of the little stray fibers. To do so, lightly moisten them and roll them around in your palm or on a clean area of your work surface. If you get stray fibers in your scroll designs, remove the fibers quickly with tweezers. If you don't get them out before the paint dries, they will be permanently embedded in your plate.

6 Paint Orange Yellow swirl

I then switched to Orange Yellow, intertwining new swirls with the previous ones.

7 Transition colors

After using two shades of each color, choose a transition color to blend with the next color family. Here I'm using Orange creating a transition to Cherry Red, Garnet Red and Ruby from the yellow swirls.

8 Develop design

If you aren't sure how to develop your own design, tap out a pattern before you start filling it in. If you don't like it, use a paper towel and turpentine to remove it and start again.

9 Stipple in scrolls

Stipple in the scroll with Leaf Green.

10 Add darker green

Next add Green scrolls intertwined with the Leaf Green scrolls.

11 Mix transition color

To ease the transition contrast between the yellows and the greens, mix an intermediate green to fill the space between them. I mixed one part Light Yellow to one part Green.

12 Finish green

After the green section is finished, the service charger is nearing completion.

13 Finish scroll design

Finish the scroll design by adding in the Sevres Blue, Lavender and Mauve scrolls.

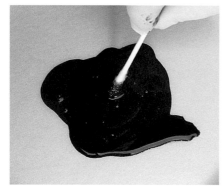

14 Mix transition color

Mix one part Garnet Red to one part Sevres Blue to make the transition color between the purple and red scrolls.

15 Add gloss glaze

After you have finished the design, allow the service charger to air-dry completely. Finish by brushing on two light coats of clear gloss glaze or even a nonyellowing polyurethane.

Variations

Want a great way to accessorize your new chargers? Use the same technique to create a colorful cake plate and dome or design matching goblets for a dramatic table setting.

Summertime Basketweave Pitcher

Treat yourself to more iced tea and lemonade with this beautiful summertime pitcher. This project teaches you how to create a basketweave pattern using matte and gloss paints to give the illusion of depth. Add delicate vines and flowers and you'll have a pitcher perfect for lazy summer afternoons.

Materials

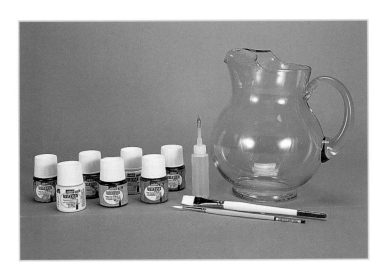

Pébéo Vitrea 160
- Azure (frost)
- Bengal Pink (gloss)
- Cloud (frost)
- Oriental Green (gloss)
- Pepper Red (gloss)
- Veil White (gloss)

Loew-Cornell White Nylon Brushes
- Series 795 no. 3 round
- Series 797F no. 6 flat stain

- glass pitcher
- 1 package Pebeo Applicator Bottles
- glass cleaner or rubbing alcohol
- latex makeup sponge
- paper towels or soft cotton rags

Difficulty:

Cost: $$

Time: ⬇ ↕

1 Clean painting surface

Thoroughly clean painting surface with glass cleaner.

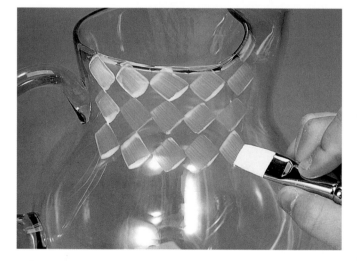

2 Paint matte diamonds

Use your no. 6 flat stain brush and Cloud frost to paint diamonds as if they were really squares set on their tips. Paint a band of diamonds three diamonds tall. Make sure you brush only in one direction. In this case, I only brushed down. At the bottom of the pitcher, paint another border of diamonds two diamonds tall.

Finished matte diamond borders

Completed upper and lower diamond borders

3 Paint glossy diamonds

Using your no. 6 flat stain brush and Veil White (gloss), fill in the open diamonds. Start with your brush at the bottom of the diamond and brush upward. The brush-strokes should be opposite those of the Cloud diamonds, reinforcing the basketweave look.

4 Add blue bands

Using your no. 6 flat stain brush, add bands of Azure (frost) at the bottom of the top diamond band, above the lower diamond band and at the base below the lower diamond band.

5 Draw vines

Fill an applicator bottle half full with Oriental Green and attach a fine metal tip. Draw vinelike stripes on an angle from the top blue band to the middle blue band.

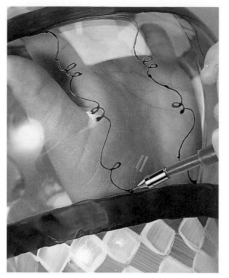

Close-up of vine stripes

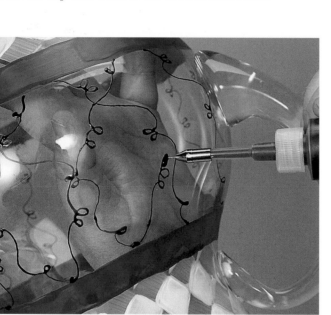

6 Crisscross vines

Repeat the process (step 5) in the opposite direction, crossing the stripes.

7 Begin flowers

Use your no. 3 round brush to paint tiny flowers in Bengal Pink and Pepper Red near the intersection of the vines. The flowers are started by making a small spiral.

8 Complete flowers

To complete each flower, make two short strokes on either side of the bottom of the spiral. Use the applicator bottle to squeeze out two short leaves.

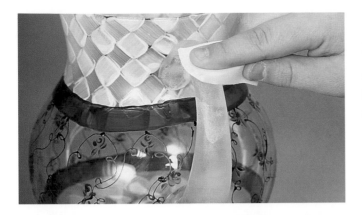

9 Decorate handle

To decorate the handle, first sponge Cloud to cover the entire handle. Finish embellishing the handle with spiral flowers, green leaves and vines, repeating elements from steps 5-8.

10 Heat-cure paint

Once you have finished painting, allow the pitcher to air-dry per paint label instructions. After it has dried place it in a cold oven. Turn your oven on to 325°F (160°C) and heat-cure your piece for forty minutes. When the baking process is complete, allow it to cool with the oven before removing it to avoid cracking.

Variation

Use the same paints and techniques from the pitcher to create coordinated goblets.

Blue Skies Candle Votive

Pefect for a rainy day, this blue sky candle votive will brighten any room. Made with paint markers, this project can be completed in a matter of minutes. Put these votives around your home and bring the sunshine indoors!

Materials

EK Success ZIG Painty Markers
- Blueberry
- Gold
- Lavender (optional for a dusky look)
- Tropic Blue
- White

- glass candle votive
- glass cleaner
- nail polish remover
- nonyellowing polyurethane
- paper towels
- cotton swabs

Difficulty:

Cost: **$**

Time:

Hint

If you don't like your design, use nail polish remover to easily wipe the design off with a cotton swab or paper towel and start again. To create a dusk effect, add a little bit of Lavender in with the blue in step 3.

1 Clean painting surface

Thoroughly clean surface with glass cleaner.

2 Paint border

Using the Gold Painty marker, color in the top band of the votive.

3 Add blue

Using the Blueberry and Tropic Blue markers, press the primed markers down on the glass, allowing them to bleed a small puddle of each color.

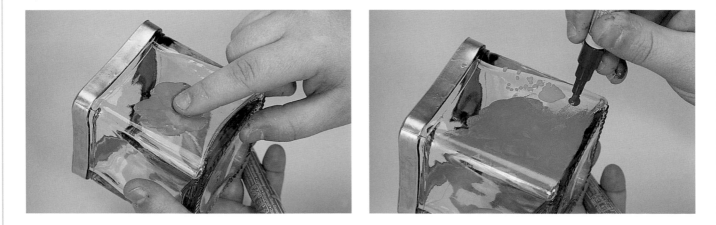

4 Cover votive with color

Working quickly, use your finger to pat and dab the marker colors over the glass surface. Completely cover the votive.

5 Complete coverage

Repeat the process until the glass votive is covered all the way around with a mottled blue background.

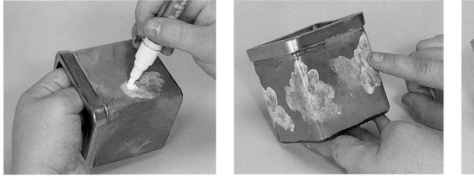

6 Begin clouds

Begin making clouds with your White marker. Make clouds by bleeding dots of White paint from the marker and patting them into a cloud shape with your fingers. Dabbing the marker tip on the cloud will also add depth to your cloud.

7 Dab in highlights

After you have dabbed on the initial cloud coat, let it dry for five minutes. Use the marker to dab in highlights on the clouds.

8 Add polyurethane

Once the votive is completed, allow it to air-dry per paint label instructions. Once it is dry, you can brush on a coat or two of nonyellowing polyurethane for added scratch resistance.

Cordial Glasses

Used for a popular dessert course option, these heart-embellished cordial

glasses are the perfect accompaniment to a romantic dinner and dessert.

These petite glasses are also wonderful for sorbets or parfait desserts.

Materials

Pébéo Vitrea 160
- Amaranthine (gloss)
- Azure (frost)
- Bengal Pink (gloss)
- Iridescent Medium

Pébéo Porcelaine 150
- Gold (44)

Loew-Cornell Mixtique Brush
- Series 8000 no. 3 round

- 4 cordial glasses
- glass cleaner
- paper towels or soft cotton rags

Difficulty: 🖌🖌

Cost: $$

Time: ⟲

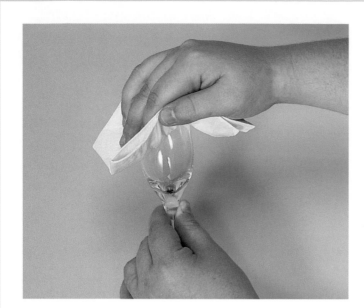

1 Clean painting surface

Clean the painting surface with glass cleaner and paper towels.

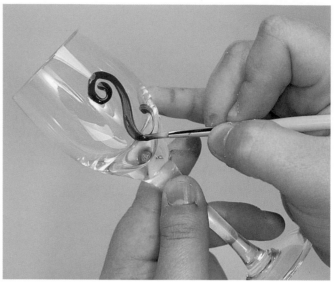

2 Paint heart

Starting 1" (3cm) from the top of the flute, paint the right side of the heart by making a small scroll then making a backwards S. Repeat this in reverse to finish the heart. Use your no. 3 round brush and Bengal Pink.

3 Paint streamer

Starting at the top of the stem paint a streamer that curls around the stem to the base of the glass.

4 Extend streamer

Where the streamer from the stem meets the base of the glass, extend the streamer into a long curl on the base of the glass.

5 Paint second heart

Paint another heart on the other side of the glass with Amaranthine. Paint in matching streamers on the stem and base that cross over the Bengal Pink streamers.

6 Highlight pink strokes

Highlight the Bengal Pink S-strokes with Amaranthine.

7 Highlight purple strokes

Highlight the purple S-strokes with Bengal Pink.

8 Paint accent

Paint a three-stroke accent in Azure with your no. 3 round brush. Begin with a long stroke going straight down centered over the heart. Then add a smaller, slightly curved stroke on each side of the long stroke, creating a fan shape. All three strokes should meet at the bottom.

9 Add dots

Dip the end of your brush in Gold and use it to make a dot at the point where the three blue strokes come together.

10 Paint border

Using Gold and your no. 3 round brush, paint a border of comma strokes around the top edge of the cordial glass. Curve one stroke up and curve the next down, overlapping slightly all the way around the rim of the glass.

11 Highlight design

Using your no. 3 round brush and the iridescent medium, highlight the heart, streamers and blue fan detail.

12 Heat-cure paint

Once your design is complete, allow the paint to air-dry per paint label instructions. Then place it in a cold oven and turn the oven to 325°F (160°C). Bake the glass for forty to forty-five minutes. Allow the piece to cool with the oven. Once the baking process is complete, the glass is dishwasher safe.

$\mathcal{K}$oi Fish Tray

This stunning koi fish serving tray utilizes dimensional glass paint to create the texture of running water and a layering effect with koi fish to create a beautiful work of art. Perfect as a unique home decor accessory for your coffee table, this tray is sure to become a conversation piece.

Materials

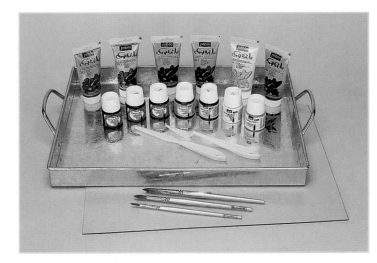

Pébéo Gel Crystal
- Iridescent (clear) (44)
- Iridescent Blue (42)
- Iridescent Green (43)
- Sapphire Blue (15)
- Sevres Blue (14)

Pébéo Liquid Crystal Paints
- Caramel (22)
- Crimson Red (5)
- Golden Yellow (2)
- Lemon Yellow (1)
- Orange (3)
- Scarlet (4)
- White (27)
- Matte Anti-UV Varnish

Loew-Cornell Mixtique Brushes
- Series 8000 no. 3 round
- Series 8000 no. 7 round
- Series 8000 no. 10 round

- 1 piece of tempered glass cut to fit the interior dimensions of your tray (available from any glass shop)
- galvanized steel tray
- black Sharpie marker
- offset plastic palette knives
- razor blade
- 4 blue flat glass marbles (available in the flower arranging section of your local craft store)
- glass cleaner
- paper towels

Difficulty:

Cost: $$$$$

Time: ⬇ ⬇ ⬇ ⬇

Enlarge this pattern to fit the dimensions of your tray.

1 Clean painting surface

Clean tray thoroughly using glass cleaner and paper towels.

2 Add paint

Squeeze out stripes of Sevres Blue randomly over the tray surface.

3 Add stripes of color

Add stripes of Sapphire Blue, Iridescent Blue and Iridescent Green in random patterns over the surface. Make sure not to neglect the corners.

Hint

Tips on using Gel Crystal paint

- Do not overmanipulate Gel Crystal because you may flatten the paint. If you do flatten the paint, just add more.
- If you make a mistake, allow it to dry, then use a razor blade to cut out the mistake. Cover it with new gel paint.
- Do not use a hair dryer or heat gun to dry Gel Crystal paint. Gel Crystal will shrink and crack under intense heat.
- Once Gel Crystal air-dries, it will not shrink.

4 Spread paint

Using an offset palette knife, begin to spread the Gel Crystal around, creating the choppy texture of water.

5 Apply green in corners

Use Iridescent Green in the corners to help bring out the intensity of the blue tones.

6 Create water

Use your palette knife to smooth the paint to create the choppy, uneven texture of water.

7 Add highlights

Using the clear Iridescent, add highlights to the water.

8 Blend paint

Blend in clear Iridescent to make the water shimmer.

9 Allow paint to dry

This is the finished wet tray. Allow it to air-dry undisturbed overnight.

10 Complete tray

This is the finished dry tray. Notice the gel has taken on a satin finish, with the exception of the iridescent colors. If you feel you would like to add more depth of color or texture, you can layer on more Gel Crystal.

11 Remove paint residue

Use a razor blade to remove any dried Gel Crystal residue on the sides of the tray.

12 Clean glass

Clean both sides of the tempered glass with glass cleaner and paper towels.

Hint

Working with Liquid Crystal paint
Be sure to let each coat of Liquid Crystal dry before applying the next layer of color. Liquid Crystal can crackle when layering a new layer on previous wet layers. You can use a hair dryer to speed the drying process between layers.

13 **Trace pattern**
Place paper pattern beneath glass and trace onto the glass with a black Sharpie marker.

14 **Paint in reverse**
Remove the paper pattern and turn the glass over so the Sharpie pattern is on the bottom. You will be painting in the pattern in reverse. Reverse painting can be a challenging technique to master. It is the process of working from the very top colors down to the backround colors; whereas in regular painting, you paint from the backround to the top colors. When reverse painting, occasionally tip your surface up to see your results. This allows you to see any areas you might need to improve.

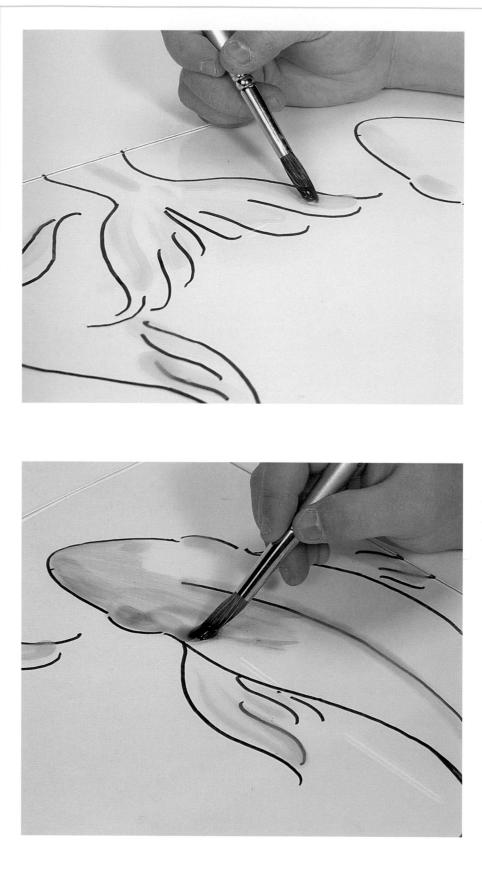

15 Paint white highlights

Using a no. 7 round brush and White Liquid Crystal paint, paint highlights over the eyes, the bottoms of the side fins, along the center spine and on the lower fins.

16 Basecoat yellow fish

Using a no. 10 round brush, basecoat the yellow fish with Lemon Yellow.

17 Basecoat orange-red fish

Use your no. 10 round brush to basecoat the orange-red fish with Orange.

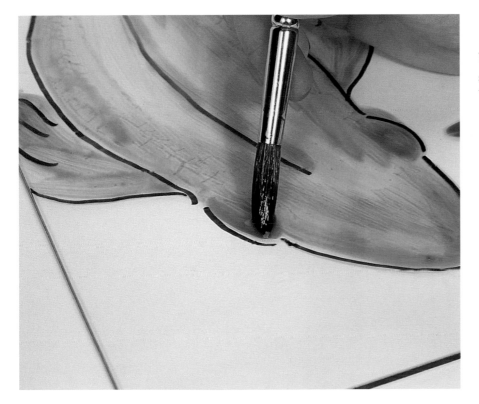

18 Shade yellow fish

Use the no. 7 round brush to start shading the yellow fish with Golden Yellow.

19 Shade orange-red fish

Shade the orange-red fish with Scarlet.

20 Shade yellow fish

Shade the yellow fish further with Orange, focusing on the edges of the nose, over the eyes and especially on the side and tail fins.

21 Shade orange-red fish

Shade the orange-red fish further with Crimson Red, focusing on the edges of the nose, over the eyes and especially on the side and tail fins.

22 Complete shading

Continue shading the yellow and red fish until they achieve dimensionality.

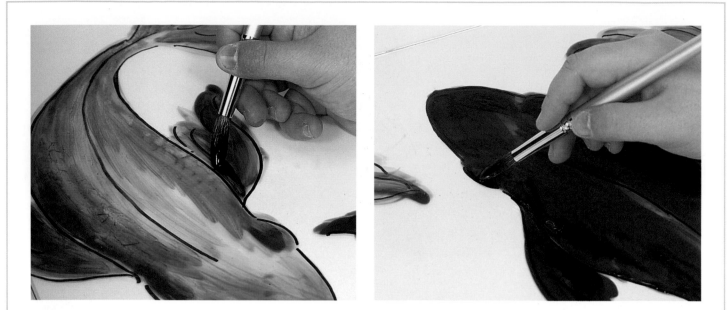

23 Add contours

Finally, add Caramel Brown to contour both colors of fish using a no. 7 round brush.

24 Paint air bubbles

Using your no. 7 round brush, paint in air bubbles with matte varnish.

25 Finish tray

When you are finished painting the glass and it is completely dry, use glass cleaner to wipe off the Sharpie marker pattern traced on the glass. To complete the tray, place the four blue glass marbles, one in each corner, to support the glass above the textured water surface. The painted side of the glass should be face down.

Photocopy these project patterns to the size that best fits your painting surface.

Use this butterfly pattern for the Flying Butterfly Soup Tureen on page 55.

©2000 Karin Burden
Atkins

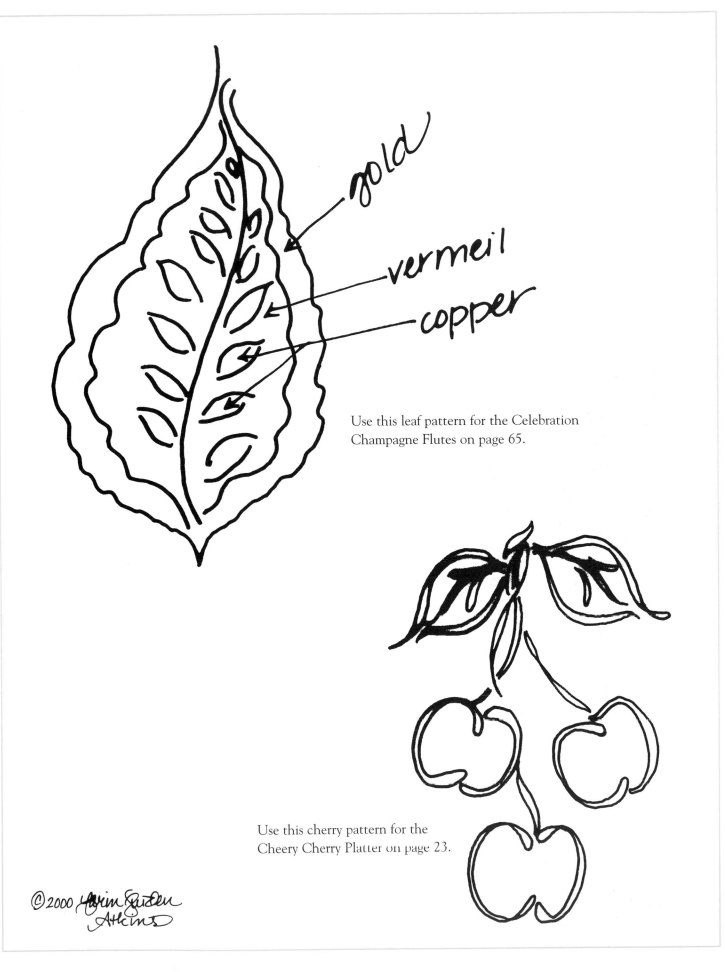

gold

vermeil

copper

Use this leaf pattern for the Celebration
Champagne Flutes on page 65.

Use this cherry pattern for the
Cheery Cherry Platter on page 23.

©2000

Now that you've leaned how to create beautiful glass and porcelain projects step-by-step, here's a gallery of inspirational ideas to spark your own creativity. Experiment with creating your own designs, and let your artistic imagination take hold!

Painted with Pébéo Porcelaine 150, these cheery cherry pieces and grape decanter are perfect for brightening up any décor. Easy to paint, these pieces use the cherry motif from the Cheery Cherry Platter (page 22), the daisies from the All-in-One Teapot (page 34) and the checkerboard technique from the Painting Techniques chapter (page 17).

Create this wonderful tea set, perfect for an afternoon tea party. Just use Pébéo Porcelaine 150 paint and review the flower technique from the All-in-One Teapot (page 34) and the stripe and scroll patterns from the Summertime Basketweave Pitcher (page 86).

This picture frame and wine goblet feature an elegant leaf motif painted with Pébéo Porcelaine 150 paint and an applicator bottle. The wine goblet stem was created using the same techniques as the Celebration Champagne Flute on page 64.

This delightful tea set was painted with Pébéo Porcelaine 150 using the stripe motif from the the Party Time Cake Plate (page 44).

These brilliant floral goblets featuring tulip petals and hydrangea blossoms were painted with Pébéo Vitrea 160 using the techniques from the Rose Goblets (page 28).

Create a whimsical keepsake piggy bank using the bouquet motif from the Lover's Teapot (page 70) and Pébéo Porcelaine 150.

These projects illustrate how you can use applicator bottles to accent finely detailed pieces. All of the pieces were painted with Pébéo Porcelaine 150.

This elegant tea set painted with Pébéo Porcelaine 150 features the same techniques used in the All-in-One Teapot (page 34) and the Summertime Basketweave Pitcher (page 86).

These acrylic plates were reverse painted on the back side of the plates with Pébéo Liquid Crystal. The paint was applied with color shapers and an applicator bottle and features the bouquet pattern from the Lover's Teapot on page 70.

This elegantly detailed place setting was painted with Pébéo Porcelaine 150. The plate and charger are reverse painted on the back side of the plates starting with the flowers to create a layered effect. A complementary wine goblet and champagne flute complete the place setting.

These garden-inspired champagne flutes were painted with Pébéo Porcelaine 150 using simple techniques such as pull daisies, comma strokes and ribbon streamers

This lovely wine glass and glass mug painted with Pébéo Porcelaine 150 use a simple floral design and stripe motif to achieve beautiful results.

This colorful geranium pitcher painted with Pébéo Porcelaine 150 features many of the techniques shown in the Painting Techniques section (page 17) such as checker-boards, pull strokes and applicator bottle techniques.

Painted with Pébéo Vitrea 160, this vivid pitcher and goblet were created with simple painting techniques and a bright color palette.

Paint Products

DecoArt
P.O. Box 327
Stanford, KY 40484
Phone: (800) 367-3047
Fax: (606) 365-9739
E-mail: paint@decoart.com
www.decoart.com

Delta Technical Coatings, Inc.
2550 Pellissier Place
Whittier, CA 90601
Phone: (800) 423-4135
Fax: (562) 695-5157
www.deltacrafts.com

Duncan
3673 E. Shields Ave.
Fresno, CA 93727
Phone: (800) 237-2642
Email: consumer@duncanmail.com
www.duncancrafts.com

EK Success
P.O. Box 1141
Clifton, NJ 07014-1141
Phone: (800) 524-1349
E-mail: success@eksuccess.com
www.eksuccess.com

Pébéo of America
P.O. Box 714
Route 78, Airport Rd.
Swanton, VT 05488
Phone: (800) 363-5012
Fax: (819) 821-4151
www.pebeo.com

Liquitex–Binney and Smith
P.O. Box 431
Easton, PA 18044-0431
Phone: (888) 422-7954
www.liquitex.com

Brushes

Loew-Cornell
563 Chestnut Ave.
Teaneck, NJ 07666-2490
Phone: (201) 836-7070
Fax: (201) 836-8110
www.loew-cornell.com

Colour Shapers

Forsline and Starr
* Forsline and Starr colour shapers can be found in local fine art and craft stores.

Porcelain and glass surfaces used in this book were from: Industrial Can Company, Pottery Barn, Crate & Barrel and Target.